Coffee Grounds for the Worm Bin

Poetry by Glenn Reed

191 Bank Street
Burlington Vermont 05401

Copyright © 2019 by Glenn Reed

All rights reserved. No part of this publication may be reproduced, distributed, or transmitted in any form or by any means, including photocopying, recording, or other electronic or mechanical methods, without the prior written permission of the publisher, except in the case of brief quotations embodied in critical reviews and certain other noncommercial uses permitted by copyright law.

Onion River Press
191 Bank Street
Burlington, VT 05401

ISBN: 978-1-949066-26-5

Library of Congress Control Number: 2019905381

Printed in the United States of America

Book and Cover Design by WillmottStudios.com

Acknowledgements

"Short Cuts" first appeared in *When it Rains From the Ground Up,* Seattle, WA.
"Piano Scales" first appeared in *Spindrift* and then in *PoetsWest,* Seattle, WA.
"Yellow Balloon" first appeared in *Knock,* Seattle, WA
"Storm" first appeared in the College of the Redwoods *2010 Poets & Writers Anthology,* Eureka, CA.
"Beyond the Fenceline" first appeared in the weekly *North Coast Journal,* Arcata, CA.
"2001: A Kubrick Night at the Accidental Gallery" first appeared in *Knock*, Seattle, WA.
Thanks to all!

This collection is dedicated to Matt and to Mom, as well as to the numerous people (many now gone) and places that have inspired my writing, including poetry, over the decades. Those people include family, friends, those I've worked with in the mental health and social services field and people I've just encountered in life on Seattle and Eureka streets, travels overseas or elsewhere. Special thanks to the poetry community in the Seattle area. When I lived there from 1994 to 2006 they helped me to develop my creative voice and motivated me to write more poetry.

All photos in this publication were taken by Glenn Reed and Matt Brennan.

Contents

I. Budding Branches 7
Dogwood Tree (at age 4) 9
Crabapple Tree (at age 6) 10
Blue Spruce (at age 8) 11
Picture Window 12
Red Maple (at age 10) 13
Elm (at age 15) 15
Footsteps 17
No Strings Attached 18

II. At the Tip of Tongue 21
Madeline's Kitchen 23
Bronze Star 25
Shortcuts 26
Waiting for the Words 28
Pastel Tints 30
Eagle Eyes 32

III. This Fragmented City 35
Piano Scales 37
Sun Spots 39
Moon Face 41
God's Favorite Crack Whore 43
Jacob's Walk 45
Intersection 47

IV. Sidewalk Cracks 49
Yellow Balloon 51
Dreaming of Martha's Vineyard 53
Men's Haircuts by Mabel 54
Storm 56
Lucky Bamboo Gift 58
The Lost Games of an Ex...... 61

V. Lost Coasts & Bare Shelves 65
Late Autumn in Humboldt 67
Dusk, Mad River Beach 68
Beyond the Fenceline 69

Spring, Red Trinities   70
Trinity River Daze   71
The Tipping Point   73

VI. Sun Showers   75
Singing Lessons   77
Outside the Boxing Tent   80
Map Folds   82
Juniper Seeds   84
The Desecration of Ursa Major   86

VII. What to Say   89
Remembering Studs Terkel   91
Anagram   92
2001: A Kubrick Night at the Accidental Gallery   94
A Free Association in White Without Knowing Spanish   96
Burying the Horse   99
The Granite Coffee House   100
Porch Gathering   102
Deja View   104
Early April   106

Notes   109

I. Budding Branches

Hold fast to dreams
For if dreams die
Life is a broken-winged bird
That cannot fly.
---From "Dreams"
by Langston Hughes

Dogwood Tree (at age 4)

        there is time
in perplexing abundance
the blinding stings from spankings
        the toot horn on mom's
            favorite record
        teasing my ears, there's
the nightlight arc swing
        at bad dreams
there is sun thirst
        and red clay crumble
        under fire ant tracks
there's the black housekeeper
        donning sky blue
at the bus stop, there
        are white bursts sipping
        Gulf air gusts, then
        spreading them across Georgia
the salt and currents
drawing open, coating lips, there's
        the lawn mower pass
            of my dad
        showering blades of grass
        stabbing at my eyes, there's
        the rubbing, the pain
the flaming afterimage,   there are the white petals
            drifting downward

Crabapple Tree (at age 6)

Stunted growth channeled to
    spindly branches
    taunting at pointless climbs
    no temptation with
this warty skin, brown mottled
    fruit--inedible

Disgruntled bodyguard
slumming with sidewalk cracks
    gorging on spring percolation
        of groundwater
    and forgotten winter melt

Plopping useless curses
    of its frustration
on the wide-eyed bluets
    violets and dandelions
    frolicking in swaths of spring sun
        beneath it

I'll toss its stones
    at my first targets
but I'll test my own limbs
    on the sturdy boughs
    of the brooding hemlocks nearby

I'll hold fast to mother's arm
    as time begins to define
        the initial wobbles
    without training wheels

I'll fall to the ground
    where the fruits of its labor
offer my first bitter path
    of random obstacles
    across a Massachusetts landscape

Blue Spruce (at age 8)

ornamental
non-native
stationary point
  of balance
cylindrical hoarder
  of branches
gyrations to arctic currents
that crackle in songs
  of icicle growth
  welcomed by reclusive boughs
wearing of sun's knowledge
  in rapid-fire sparkles
sanctuary of powder's levity
  until the sky burdens
  their space with lessons
    and they thump to the ground
    laden with the experience
defining space, but
I can't know your height
  or explore your scented depths
I walk past you to second grade
books balanced under
  one arm
lessons seeking subject, predicate
  and object, a new math of
adding in the sprouting of
    carrot and radish seeds
subtracting the burning of toys and
    nights of
  tear-filled, swollen eyes
multiplying one times one
  times two times
the needles, seasons,
  years

Picture Window

Mt. Ascutney scratched
    flecks of winter
    from the sky overnight
A wind spread this impulse
    across the fields laid outstretched
    beyond our picture window
Mother looks out, sipping
    her morning tea, the steam rising
    past her gaze and away
    from my questions
    paused under the doorframe

What do you see? I form the words
    but they choke in a silence

What do you want to see?

A monadnock
a lone peak
new snow coating
the bare spots on its granite summit

Slowly she begins to turn
November is watching
    over her shoulder

Red Maple (at age 10)

We settled into a perch of hills
we watched the neighbor's two horses
nibble away the grasses
to reveal Mt. Ascutney's stab at
the meandering cloud drift

One horse was brown, the other white
I somehow remember their names—
Frosty and Velvet--
they herded our yard, within the washboard
dirt road, the depression of swamp muck
on one side, behind was the cascade of birch
drifting down the back hill in meditation with
the soft, green hush of bracken fern

We framed the four seasons there
my mother's steeping of tea bags
fogging up her *"have a good day at school"* window
later, with the crash of our sleds, my brother and I
bounced up and over insistent winter drifts
landing, with stars dancing
under the breezeway awning

The winter's aurora borealis danced as orange curtains
the maples tapped a song that later burned
upward in puffs of sugar house steam
dissipating in the crinkled night air
the flash floods of late spring
funneled tales of abandoned farms on glacial till

The television strained for reception
the hay fields in summer begged for cutting
the mudroom door creak-whispered
of tv dinners and hard slammings

The red maple's leaves
rushed with scarlet
presenting us with autumn questions
in the midst of summer lethargy
knowing we'd be gone
from there
all too soon

Elm (at age 15)

Before moving in
        the former owners told us:
"This is the largest elm in the State of Vermont."
        and the limbs were then relieved of this back road
knowledge
        and so soon began to fall

Before moving in
        and the dimensions were defined clearly
the elm branches began to beg for
        handfuls of cloud and earth

And during our first summer there
        the storm clouds billowed with the turning of soil
the voices cracked, tongues dried
        in the speaking of corn and sweet clover
        and the taste of slow decay

And as we tossed our dreams, our thoughts, our arguments
        beneath the welcome hug of leaf and hair tussle
We felt the dab of constellations
and the distraction of killdeer "dee-dee-dee"ing
        across summer haze and dusk sky, past hay field
past the crossing of our grass-stained shoes
        through hallway walls inscribed with names
        we didn't think we knew

Finding our own spaces, we embraced each room
        filled closets with a fold of clothes creased
        with secrets written on crumpled notes
        and stuffed into pockets
We sat on the front porch
        with eyes peeled for lightning bugs
occasionally blinded by the sweep of headlights
        from cars rumbling down our dirt road
        that drowned out the easy, firefly flickers

After settling in, I froze my limbs

sweltered under summer night sheets, strained
to hear the whine, feel the vibration
    of nearby passing trains speeding paths
through the pitch black, where a blanket of hardwoods
    spread down from the foothills

I began counting rings, tracing the contours
    of river shaped valley, attached my hopes
to railroad ties, zippering my youth
    to a convergence point
    sucked into the distant mountains
    that drew the railroad line to the north

And I began leafing through pages in scrapbooks
    wondering at the black and white toddling
    of my mother
down a street where a row of elms lay
like pick-up straws, scattered by the hurricane of '38
    and stepfather, scrunched in the yellowing
    corner of a class photo from the 4th grade

Because after we moved and settled in
the thunder growled of the future
    while I counted the seconds from lightning
to booming, as each tree ring
wrapped its way around another year
    and the flash of knowledge, posed questions
    with often harsh answers

Because after we moved and settled in,
the largest elm in the state
    began to fall, even as I acknowledged its patterns
of decay, then helped stack the remains
    in the back of our pick-up
    to be carted away

And as we settled in, and the summer grew tired
    prepared its bed in a harvest of the corn
    and the blush and fall of leaves
The largest elm in the state quietly made way
    for a larger patch of sky

Footsteps

footsteps pass my room, maybe mom
checking on the sunday roast, the oven
having sizzle and crackled it to well-done
after mother stood her ground at church with the choir

footsteps, could be our company weekending
the great, wild northlands, that stretched their limbs
from the spine of route 5's four lanes
jabbing forth shopping centers and november hunting season
motel rates, hot turkey sandwiches a special
plateful at the brown carpet restaurants, featuring
local artists taking shelter under the ubiquitous
covered bridges

footsteps, that could be my stepfather pondering
the appropriate time for me to split wood
into cords of energy savings, gas lines still
meandering down the dirt road, or when to chip off
the sub-freezing settling of the previous night
in the horses' water buckets, the time for me
to un-bale rectangles of summer haying
from just three months prior
toss them into the stalls, let the horses chew and
taste of runs through fields of timothy and clover

footsteps, they backtrack to the kitchen as I
turn a leaf of albert camus, wring out the words that
march in roman type across the brown hillside, spell out
the yellowed fields, stubbled with nubs of felled cornstalks
I'm almost seventeen and count the rows
that lead me to the guillotine
where camus says we all kneel, we all raise the ax
and split wood stove fuel for the fires
that will always burn, warming near-winter days
turning pages until the footsteps return and I think
I already know who will eventually be knocking

No Strings Attached

I squint, now, looking for thin tendrils
   to grasp as my thoughts percolate
Like carbonation, at times, or a slow
   fermentation, in other moments
But now, ascending the amber liquidity
   of an anguished moment

If I focus, they'll slow, I'll lasso
   a bubble, ride this globular
Belch of gas, rise
   towards the foaming mass
   seconds, decades and
   eons above

There I'll grab a number and
   wait my turn for release
   to neon-lit, but blurred
Mapscapes after all, no one
   ever said there would be
   no strings attached

Grandpa, when I was just age nine
   advised me to never indulge
In drink, his words imprinted
   like dancing fish scales
   beached on crinkled, onion-skin paper
So I circled the wagons
   'round to keep from taking
   this ride

Mom, around the same time
   whispered in my ear not to
Pull the curtain cord, but squeeze
   instead, the umbilical cord, only
The oxygen seeped out
   from between the folds of
Her closed drapes, revealing

    a chamber bathed in that
    familiar, honey thick light

Back when I was four, Suzanne
    a neighbor who was six and hard-of-hearing
Handed me a string of consonants
    leading to an inflated vowel
The color of bronze, a letter, round, of
    obese plastic, helium-filled
"Hold tight to the string!" Mom reminded me
    thus opening the summer haze above
    to the sentence forming on my lips

But the balloon escaped my distracted fingers
"Oooh!" Suzanne giggled, waving hands upward
    the letter "O" imbedding in the sky above
And her meandering laugh
    a wind on the puff clouds
    as the balloon rose
    and floated on, string dangling

Grandma always used to
    mail me newspaper clippings
    stamp-licking the thread of years
When I was eight, one was a story
    of a little boy carried aloft
    by a clustered bloom of balloons
Their strings writhing and wrapped
    'round his thin wrists

A thousand feet he rose
then higher, floating above
The elms, succumbing to disease
    the surrounding hills
    molded by slow erosion, two
    thousand feet, three thousand,
    and rising more
Until a random parachutist
floated by, like a milkweed seed

    on the wind and he
    nabbed the finger painting child
    back down to Earth, but no one

Believes me about
    this story any more, and I never saved
    those clippings
Grandma is long-gone too, but
The *"Ooooooooh....!"* laugh of Suzanne
    is still audible, tickling at
    my calloused skin and my eardrums
    with no strings attached

II. At the Tip of Tongue

Madeline's Kitchen

Grandma Madeline's kitchen rebels
        under a thumb of summer dusk
everything is crackling and spitting
        despite her calculated caresses

Hot dogs, split length-wise
        roll angrily in cooking oil
home fries sizzle competition
        with the radio static, coughing out
        the approach of a thunderstorm

Grandma's Tareyton cigarette
        reclines haughtily
        on the ashtray curb, its smoke
casually curls, seeking escape
        through a screen window

The curtains beg for a cool sweep
        of breeze over the sink
where the suds pop with impatience
        exposing the greasy film of morning dishes

Grandma Madeline demands order
        twists the radio dial with knowing fingers
to nab a polka, that happily swirls
        through her rebellious domain

She apprehends the dinner rolls
        crouched in the breadbasket
sets them on the table, where
        they flirt with a stick of oleo

Grandma pauses, gazes out the window
        towards the brick bastion of mill
where Grandpa's limbs still lurch and creak
        and routines bark their urgency

She catches the peal of child's play "down street"
        and the desperation of teenage tires seeking
to recompose the meltdown of sun
        and tries to gently rock this tendril of moments

Grandma hums clarinet glee to the bathroom
        her refuge of q-tips, baby oil, and aspirin
stares at the mirror, then rinses off her questions
        before returning to finish preparing yet
        another meal, with the four walls and
        bingo card years subdued, once more

Bronze Star

bronze—a color sheared off dusk
by winter-sharpened tongues of cloud

bronze—a color oozing in the peanut butter jar, full of
home-made syrup,
tasting of gnarled, sugar maples

bronze—like flaking page bits
from the old family bible, passed on
and on

bronze—the color of wallpaper having breathed in
stifled lives,
now peeling with rasps and wheezes

bronze—like the star, the old photo and article, now shellacked
to a piece of wood,
that once leaned on grandma's enclave of knick-knacks and
proud memories

a color of your service under fire, from the forgotten war,
passed on to me after her triple bypass
and final strokes

bronze—a melt of butterscotch sauce on what grandma might
have thought just dessert
or an amber stare through tepid beer

bronze—yellowing the pages, with the mortar-fired words, and
the frozen handshake from a captain

dad, just where are your words of farewell in this bronze star
afterglow,
in this newspaper clip bit of memory?

maybe we're all just casualties
of life's friendly fire

Shortcuts

Mom liked to take shortcuts
point A to point B
evolving into a
lesson in geometry

She'd reset the odometer
the way she would deal
the gin rummy cards
tasting the run or three-of-a-kinds
like the jolt
from that first sip of vodka

Sometimes we'd gain a few miles
in these meanders
yet lose several minutes
the distance savings dust-clouding
behind the car or
scraped off plates like dinner debris
from more turn-arounds than in
a game of blind man's bluff

My brother and I, anxious for
the trips to conclude
would roll our eyes, dial our friends in thought
smack base hits towards
the often unfamiliar scenery

We'd whine with the descent
of the power windows, little interest
in the old millstones our mother spied
grinding in some oak-shaded undergrowth
we'd fidget with the frenzy
of the deer she pointed at, startled
at field edges where they nibbled leaves
near calving stone walls

These short-cuts sewed patches
on long-worn days and the habits

she would shake and mix, like oil in vinegar
to tang her salads

Wearing this spontaneity today
I'll still thread a day's needle
with routes unknown, kick, like mother
at the comfort of mundane, still
take a quick turn down an unfamiliar dirt road
to curl my way to home, savoring the voyage
like the ribbon
on an unwrapped present

Waiting for the Words

I watch her nimble fingers sliding
     through the tangle of blackberry thorns
     plucking corpulent fruit
thoughts on the berry soup she would make

A subdued disk of sun
     sighs through murky skies, and lake weed weaves
in the froth that lingers
     where the waves murmur of August laziness
     on the shore

We sift beach sand through liberated toes
     beneath a white pine canopy
and the muggy air rouses beads of sweat
     that plaster t-shirts to skin

Later, the afternoon pressures my feet
     on the bicycle pedals, as I gulp the humidity
nestle my body into the lay of the rolling, Maine landscape
     then hunch, aerodynamic and cooling, to
     wheel into porch chair villages

I'm encircling the lake, and you
     become a diminishing point, on a bristled jaw of land
where I know you wring the last from the weekend
     with beach towel, and bookmark it with Jane Smiley

After returning, I'm chopping carrots for dinner salad
     watch you rinse the berries and tumble them in
the colander to drip, and I wonder at the benign creep
     of dusk and the lone robin commentary

After soup and salad we stretch on the comforter
     and notice Redford's middle-aged furrows
     on the tv screen
then break, amidst cricket chorus, to stroll to the dairy bar
     where the ice cream sinks quickly
     into the sugar cone funnels

Your tongue skims at maple smoothness, nabs stray walnuts
       but I still pick at bits of blackberry seed
       between my teeth
at a loss for words beyond the opening lines
       I scribble, where you're picking and plopping
       into a bucket
the substance of this Sunday and I notice the red smear
       on your palm and wonder if it's a berry stain
       or the pinch of coming realities

The lines stretch with twenty-plus years now
       down that undulating stretch of Route 302
I can still only bite at the seeds, never spit them out
       and I'd never tasted cold berry soup before
              that lingering, summer evening

Pastel Tints

The screen door "whap"
        launches your amble to the garden
        where you'll yank weeds
and nab some snap peas for dinner
        under the bow of sunflowers
        weighted to August surfeit
            with the placid, blue sky feast

The summer afternoon meanders
        its breezes rarely roused
        to ruffle the landscape
the hours seem to drift down a mellow stream
        where my hands are cottonwood branches
        poised to loosen leaves from the bank
            into a fluttering dance to the water surface

They test the current, savor
        the glint of sun speckles
        and the eventual sinking
            to the gravel bed

I turn, glance to where you'd sat
        the steam still curls
        from a mug full of peppermint tea
            lingering, like your comma hint of smile
            between tentative sips

I want to tell you how I savor
        steeping the leaves, tasting your
            gaze from the shade
            along that stream bank
How I
        caress the scent of fresh dill and oregano
        squeezed between your earth-caked fingertips
how I squint my eyes less to hear
        the tint you sing from the bountiful landscape

I'm painting what I want to say
        in soft brush strokes
        as I peer out the window
now, and frame your figure
        with lupine, foxglove and California poppy

You offer that right touch of pastel
        to complete this picture at my fingertips
can I now simply breath in these moments contentedly
        without the need to add shades anymore?

Eagle Eyes

"Look over there, over there!"
  we repeat to her
      our fingers jabbing in futility,
      lost in the river bank mobbed
      by alders, celebrating early spring
      with their burst of catkins
      like a pastel confetti against
      a more reserved blue sky
      that is hungry for the
        advent of more
        discrete foliage

We try to point out the eagle to her,
      as it folds drafts of air
      and eases in sync with the Skagit River's
      blue-tinted meanderings and
      bedrock whims at being obstinate
Those patient testings of landscape
      that the eagle's white crown
      seems to highlight, trailing
      like an unplugged evening star
      then gradually swallowed in the din
        of forest and
        mountain interplay
 A speck seeking to plummet into
      the glint of salmon splash past
      the next curve, that's anchored
        by tumbled stone

We keep pointing, but
      her eyes are tired
      done with squinting at
      each signature from 85 years, like
      old curled and yellowed notes, wanting
      the dresser drawers to shut and be
      content with paperbacks at the coffee table

        below that nose-smudged
        picture window

She's tired of staring
        out on dusk-emptied driveways
        and the neighbors untrimmed hedge
She's tired of her spectacles
        forever slipping down her nose
        though she still smiles at the details
        hidden corners, a lone trillium, the fine lines
          blurred into the landscape

"Where is it?" she asks one more time,
        scanning the scene
        but the eagle is a memory in tree trunks
          and craggy, Cascade peaks
So we soon move on, feeling failure
        though she beams in the lemony filter of sunlight
        smiles at the river curving towards the
        floodplain, tulip fields, and Skagit Bay
Thanks us for the drive,
        never again mentioning the eagles
          we'd driven so far to see

III. This Fragmented City

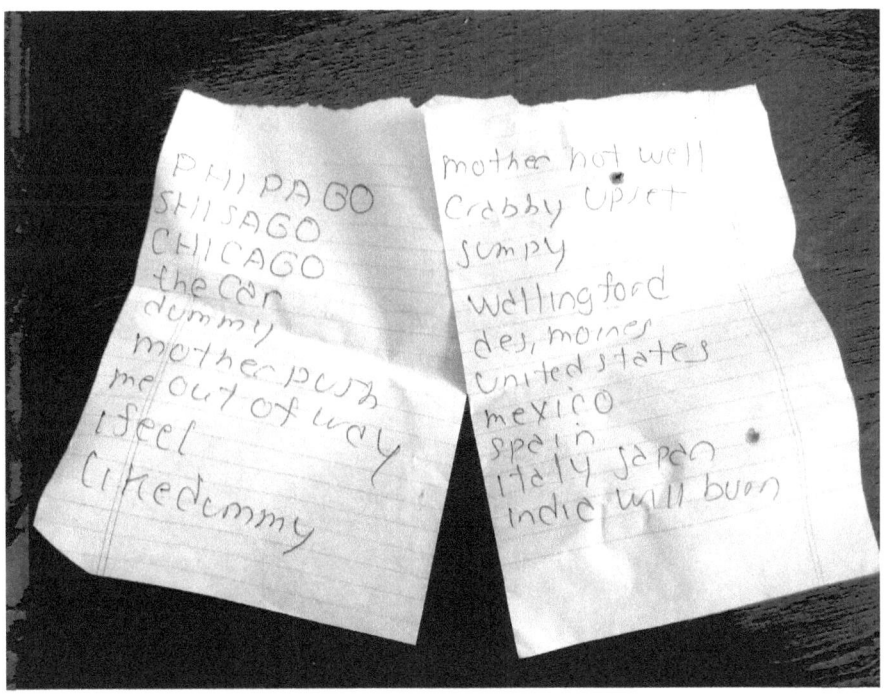

Piano Scales

Her arms are raised expectantly over the Yin-yang array
    anxious for the cool, smooth contact
    when buttery fingertips meet tonal flavors

The lamp, a sentinel beside her
    casts waves across the room
    cresting, then dropping into troughs
    they carry her in metered moments
    like rations beyond her parched tongue

Her glassy eyes meet the shadow-encrusted ceiling
    seeking an earthen coalescing of the ravaging voices
    and of the wolves that circle
    beyond the brittle lamp light

Weeks and days and hours she funnels
    into G major runs, crescendos and grace notes
    though the latticework is cut
    by razor-edged echoes over jumbled years
    and broken into puzzle shards

She tosses high-pitched admonitions
    as if proper scales could quell
    the chorus needling at her concentration
    then catches wisps of images dancing over the measures

She sees pictures held behind musical bars
    of her falling into a hole screaming *"Mama, I'm here!"*
    of her falling thousands of feet
    in millions of years

And images masquerading in a child's palm
    of her meeting God, who is clad
    in a white dinner suit, and who tells her fingers to dance
    until they curl up in cramps

So she tosses fragments of Chopin's *"Nocturne"*
    and torn sheets of Schubert
    to ride the feeble light and keep the dim room afloat
    in the ink blot sea

And under the forest canopy
    she composes dew drops on moss bedding
    while thunder cracks the horizon
    while sheets of rain reverberate her name
    over and over
     until her fingers pull away

Sun Spots

You know I once had an apartment on the surface of the sun
so I didn't worry too much about overexposure to ultraviolet light
in fact, my skin glowed with such radiance
that lipstick blotches floated like sun spots
and compact powder rode the cosmic winds
erupting from my pores

Nor did I fear sunstroke, given my chumminess with the landlord
so while coasting on our morning pleasantries
and heartfelt *"good evenings"* I decided to follow
a glimmering tassel, drifting down
the northern California coastline
combing out Highway 1's hairline curves
I oiled the convergence of tires to asphalt fingertips
shielding my eyes from shimmering sun wedges
cut by the Pacific horizon

It was then that I was waved over by meditative police
who carefully questioned me on the nature of my solar residency
and asked for the flaring details from my lease
while affording me the vinyl expanse
of their cruiser's back seat
and the elastic comfort of a stick
of Wrigley's spearmint chewing gum

They became so engrossed in my story
that they neglected to stay on the bridge
which spanned a stream issued forth
by the oak-embroidered hills
and we sailed forth, siren wailing, into wave froths
then sank quickly beneath the sea, just dead weight, a
Detroit-assembled relic of heavy metal,
dropping downward beneath the roiling skin
of this tidal illusion

This detour, I think, is listed by Rand McNally
as the national scenic byway to Atlantis

but one officer whispered to me *"it's the station!"* as he parked,
opened the door, and invited me to wade to the lab
where men in white frocks pinned with sea urchins
swept the sandy floors clean
and proclaimed to me, with much fanfare
"Here is where you invented that morsel of gum!"

I'm chewing on this now as I slump in the embers of this chair
with my *"Born Free"* rendition eclipsed
by this stark moon of residency
and as I pivot my capsule around I just see
figures mouthing lyrics that I can't hear
what is this place anyway,
some kind of wax museum?

Now I can't even order a goddamned V-8 to toast this corona
and my ex rides some back roads
in a broken down Chevy Citation
I remember the last time he dropped by
he bought me a box of Raisinets
at some movie about a ship sinking
I think it was the Titanic

And now my daughter's lost like that busload of children
I drove through the barren woods, back in Jersey
she called me from Memphis the other day
and said she'd send a post card
from Graceland, you know, I used to be Janis Joplin
'til I jumped from that window
and the pearls unhooked from my necklace
and rolled down into the gutters

And did I tell you I once had an apartment
on the surface of the sun?
and I didn't worry at all about the light blinding me
maybe I can check out the *Rolling Stones* classifieds
or *Seattle Times*, maybe I'll see if it's listed there
before the mascara drips from my eyes
and the hand lotion evaporates
from this fragmenting city

Moon Face

button o'moon
how's it your
silky blue light whips on past
them thousands of miles
like nothin'
then pools, layin'
in my paths like
a dozin' dog

crazy moon,   enticin' me so
damned fickle bowl of cream
don't know when you'll curdle
just workin' your ways
with that whisper to your
stardust cohorts
sprinklin' sugar on this road
this here path of cold concrete

moon face
so full of yourself
you know how I tire
you know I'm sick to hell
of you muckin' up
my path, draggin' your fingers
'cross my saggin' eyelids
poppin' open my suitcase to
scatter my clothes behind, like cotton 'n polyster
crumbs, lettin' you spotlight
my stagger
and fall

mockin' moon
spillin' the glitter
from them pockets and pores
then settlin' on this chasm
of floor creaks
rememberin' them days when I hung up high

in that dark velvet dress of sky
on your hook of crescent
then later on in the month
you cool with my grovel
and ticklin' my brow
as I scraped my forehead on the floor
sniffin' hard
for some lost specks of
your silver dust
perfume

you there, harsh moon
with them thousands of faces
and moods
flickerin' routes towards
your scarecrow stares
shovin' me under streetlights
the future 'n past whizzin' by
zappin' my hopes on neon motel signs
like a flame-craving insect

beckon on, moon
your icy gleam
drawin' me on to final bows
and *"thank you m'ams!"*
with eyes tossin' gazes into that gulf
splashin' with the heaven
you summon forth
in a squeezin' of distance
shimmerin' in the waves below

oh, wise-ass moon
sayin' you'll finally
teach me
how to swim

God's Favorite Crack Whore

God writes prescriptions
his cursive winding like a crackhead's
graffiti, swerving beneath
the finger-pointing of the streetlights
and looping its way into the alcove behind
the 24-hour laundromat, and the alley between
section 8 hot plates, cooking bright ideas
in smashed lightbulbs, inhaling the scent
of dried piss on brick
and first of the month

God drops a bauble into the hand
of his *"favorite crack whore,"* motions her
up the fire escape that hangs
by his word, creaks with leaden feet
of this gospel through Pauls, Johns and Jesus
in a sandal-donned trod of desert
undulations of filthy mattress, branding her back
with sacred images, the sound of daddy
slamming the good book
on beer-puddled tv trays with that first
one-way free ticket
ride to pain

"You've been saved!" miracles at one slow
injection of bus stop, midnight arrivals
after daddy stuck her on the non-stop, chanting
of seats reserved for Hare Krishnas, and of
saviors that would crawl up her scarred legs,
spread before her
in that promised land, scattering
in puddles of cheap and red, spilled
from the clutch of wrinkled, brown sacks
invisible pestilences that gurgled in voices,
hoarse and sticky
driving her silken locks of hair
into splinters that imbedded in
a specter of barren soil

"How's my favorite crack whore?"
dribbled from God's chapped lips, fissuring
the back streets cooking in the underpass where her
bared feet padded in cold run-off, just for something to feel
pan-handling love, a donut, a can
of pop, a burn and a lit-match memory
of a warm summer day and those same feet
dangling off a dock
lapped by mountain lake waters
comforting, cool, placid, hearing her mother's suggestion
to just dip them in, to...

"Just try it honey, just try it. Just once…."

Jacob's Walk

the cold sniffing at
your padded footsteps
your plans
shoeless in faith
unbuttoned before
the gawking night
sandal treads seeking
a path over sock holes

steps toward freedom from
the buzzing open of
doorways, from bread
blanched of
the taste of preparation

it's all a wandering
to the oasis, a haven
a sanctuary, a place
of worship, nourished
with sips of candlelight

but the false gods cower
and scurry past, growl
in bass voices, scream
epithets, spew exhaust
in their rage
at this naked faith
this tousled hair

the cold breathing
hard, baring its
sharp, crystalline teeth
into choice hypotheses
into faith and healing

the stars mocked in
blue flashes and commercial

break volume, voices insisting
that you've usurped this name
this name...Jacob

the frost settles
the foliage cringes
the asphalt sparkles
with light rain and streetlights

you answer, once again
to guttural voices that demand
"keep your hands to yourself!"

Intersection

Hey, yeah
gated, shopping list stare
I know I should *"get a job!"* your
tires always spin those custom hubs
and tired clichés down my unmarked
back roads, safely off the map

Yeah, I write on corrugated cardboard
a tear of some back alleyway
bleeding in black marker, burned
rubber and
late adolescent bruised letters
spelling out titles
of required readings

So here, where we intersect
the asphalt radiates afternoon heat
and your pat judgements
from vinyl thrones, your eyes
pull my bootstraps tight
raise old welts, salt the wounds
beneath the thrift store faded jeans
and too-tight shoes

You know, you wouldn't last a mile
in them anyway
and your spare change
isn't worth the idling thoughts
that disperse with
the green light, indifferent fart
of exhaust clouding the six lanes
to the horizon, look

From here it's all advice
leaked in distant spills
and impaled childhoods, with your
foot on the gas, denying
any fault lines, hey….
I'll get a job if, just once,
you truly open your eyes

IV. Sidewalk Cracks

Yellow Balloon

Dear daughter,

> I'm sitting by the picture window
> there remains a lone, yellow balloon
> a bauble, forgotten party favor
> leaking away the last
> of its round, breathed festivity
> in the viburnum bush
> an occasional breeze taunts
> its decay to this bladder shape
> and final, limp resignation

Dear daughter,

> I'm diminished by this window
> while munching on leftover macaroni salad
> with its hint of flavors
> of garden mint
> and yesterday's family gathering
> framed here
> and of the grandkids cheering hits beyond
> all of the yard's boundaries

Dear daughter,

> the Pooh Bear house you coaxed
> from packing boxes, duct tape
> and paint set memories
> still holds that silly bear's patient watch
> for a four year-old's wonder-filled eyes
> and home run innings
> to bound around the corners
> birthday cake candles still lit

Dear daughter,

> it's the same, steamy cup of tea
> moistening my forehead

today as yesterday morning
though I stirred in a dab of honey
mixed it with the cursive
of these words
I massage onto paper
this card that spoke of you
this dew grass snapshot
before midday sun
I wish I'd taken so many times
when you showed me your crayon drawings
or added this sprig of mint
to the salad,
but I was distracted

Dear daughter,

so many tasks overlooked in the preparations
and in the clean-up after such gatherings
so many good-byes crammed into the car backseats
and between ferry schedules
left hanging on the bushes never pruned

Dear daughter,

my fingers ache
with the mere lift of this pen
the pinch of summer traffic
won't let me turn my neck
far enough
from this picnic table view

Dear daughter,

please open this card
before yesterday loses its breath
the viburnum blushes red
in the embarrassment of dusk

Dreaming of Martha's Vineyard

"I see your faith and your eye for beauty reflected in his work..." *

He pictured you
tip-toeing over
the crest of waves
kneading the distant rise
of bluffs
then walking this crust of earth
with Franz Wright

He'd walk to you now
but the tide doesn't
accommodate
this perfect scenario

Somehow his words
can only float on this sea
adjective heads just above water,
his sentiments
drift down to clam beds
whisper in dark depths

there's no parting of these seas
to your Martha's Vineyard

Now three years have passed and
the raindrops patter this
used bookstore window
wrinkling pages
with these heartfelt wishes
here, both of you are authors of stories
but writers without last names

"Happy birthday, Katie!" he penned
inside this book cover

But sometimes the
many happy returns
can only
offer this pocket change
for others to spend

Men's Haircuts by Mabel

Clippings mingle on the floor
clippings,		shavings,		tints sipping
		at fluorescence and 60 watt
curls,	fine,	coarse
		and flooded with gray
shavings,		arrested growth
uniform,		sprinkled to tile
checkerboard that's pitted
		from her rotations 'round
				the barber chair

Magazines,	pondered,	flipped through
the ad deflecting eyes with gloss
		to the slink of fog outside,	lady draped
scent of cologne,		hormones no match for
		downshifting momentum of 18-wheel
		freight stroke of this strand
				of the 101

Nicotine,		taking refuge in her blouse
purple,		yellow,		patterns
		gaining entrance in backroom
breaks,		pulling at the oxygen tank
stirring Sanka, slipping
		into the molded cot
		reclining of decades
sweeping up the tips
		and wind-gusted
	Lost Coast afternoons

Her arthritic mutt, named Chelsea
		nose-smudging glass
coffee table top with
		two thump tail
		curiosity at necktie
		customer,	preferring
	shag carpet comfort smells

savoring the feet that have tread
      elsewhere,   the dropped
            potato chips or other bits
                 of lunch break

The mirror,   confirmation of
preparations for meetings,
weddings and funerals
peeking back at the days between
      Polaroid snaps of
trips to Las Vegas and
goodbyes to grandsons shipped
      off to Baghdad,   moments
that won't stick with scotch tape
      for too long,   clippings
      that flutter to the floor
as the scissors seek the pattern
      that will finally make everything look
          complete

Storm
(for a ceramics artist never met)

She'd felt the billowing clouds
    in cupped hands, poised to let loose
    in cumulus, puffed and oozing
    between fingertips
then, the gray mass thrown
    with the pressure
    of lost afternoon stillness

That anticipation, spun and dabbed
    with childhood's tantrums, and mid-life grieving
the tears, the frowns, a sigh
    gusting outward in puffs of clay dust

Like hints of that musty odor
    in summer attics or barns, waiting
    with the knowledge of heartbeats shaped
between blink of a flash and
    the low rumble of thundered advance
    beyond stooped ridge backs, then

That scent of ozone, like the Earth
    exhaling in shapes of pasture, oak tree and rose garden
    before the eruption of cloud

Sometimes it's in the gathering,
    or in the sheets of chaos
    written in clenched fists
Sometimes it's in the clearing sky
    roiling masses held beyond palm prints
    tentative drops tracing
    this plot of a weathered Earth
    rotating without concern

Sometimes it's in each pore, erupting
    with this satiation of the heavens
    eyes staring between thunderclaps

    feet venturing outdoors to see downed limbs
    sunflowers and gladiolas beaten into bows

Then, at last, it's in the peeking of sun
    past the next wheel spin that
    sets the droplets aglow
tracing the zig-zag of a lifeline
    across the malleable clay
waiting for the final stain
    of tears, slowed breath
    of simple contemplation

Lucky Bamboo Gift

The flyer floating on the window glass says
something about a lucky bamboo gift
      ideal for Mother's Day

And it's a Friday night at Harvard & Pike Streets
      on the Hill
but no one seems to know just what
      is a lucky bamboo gift

No answers come from above, where
a sickle moon seeks to disembowel
      the strewn tissue clouds
while it coats a fine enamel light
      on the grimy, Seattle sidewalks

No answers pulsate from the neon contrast
with the flatline emptiness
      of the storefronts, but only hint
      of a desperation writhing within

No answers, either, across the street
      where no one's permanent
at the beautician school, with its offerings
      of beheaded mannequin chorus lines
they whisper banalities, these Marie Antoinette
      wanna-be's, these retread Marky Marks and Madonnas
that smirk beneath tangles of blonde and brunette

And on the street, sewer grates steam
      futilely outward, a botched stab
      of anesthesia, seeking to tranquilize all disarray
on the opposite block, yellow fin tuna's the special
      at the Rosebud Cafe, and it's charred
      like the abstract of corners in the next-door
      art gallery, where the shadows burn
      into the nooks and onto the floor

But no one there knows just what is a lucky
        bamboo gift
        no one seems to know

No answers in the splashy shirt oratorio
        of a prancing boy toy, tangling his drama
        with the cell phone chatter, fly-papering substance
for little does the content matter
        little does it matter

Only whimpers from
        a huddled cocker spaniel
        bound to a bike rack, its drooping head staring
        at the oversized jeans mushrooming by
meanwhile its master stays glued
        to the frozen dusk of internet cafe
        his latte hot and foaming at the mouth
        as he sips the last of the day

And no one here seems to know
        just what is a lucky bamboo gift
        ideal for Mother's Day
                no one is here to ask

No one is seated at a summer morning
        window display, waving their content
        with the patio scene, sipping tepid tea
        munching stale sugar cookies
        that twinkle thoughts of flavor
        under spotlights, while they choke
                on bitter mouthfuls of crumbs

No one's feet caress the artificial grass
        ache with their weight on
        the cast iron chairs, feel the cut
        of brazen moments that felled
        the stump-shaped clear-cut of placid scenes

And further down Pike, the dome of the First Covenant Church
    belches blue light and Jesus
    at the weaving scarecrow figures
    and at the dingy bar opening doors
    on all of these unanswerable questions
Beneath its stained glass windows
    a lone iris's tongues of petal pant
    and lap at a square of earth, two-by-two hatch
    in the concrete, cut for escape, four-cornered tear
    maybe digging to nowhere, maybe
        hinting in monochrome light
        of somewhere or just elsewhere

But it's all neither
    here nor there, for
    no one knows on this hook-mooned
        Friday night
    just what is a lucky gift
    just what
is a lucky bamboo gift

The Lost Games of an Ex......

(And our teacher taught us a song today...but I forgot the melody)

and I lost all a day and I lost all a year and
I lost when to touch and I lost when to feel

> *"Raspberry, strawberry and apple jam tart*
> *Tell me the name of your sweetheart.*
> *Raspberry, strawberry and apple jam tart*
> *Tell me the name......Tell me the name..."*

When you meandered home from school for lunch
when your friends scattered for their Campbell's soup
with grilled cheese sandwiches

> *"Raspberry, strawberry and apple jam tart...."*

Apples jammed and apples fell in a fog of chalkboard dust
before being gnawed to the core, apples fell
from the teacher's lesson book, rolled
across the creaking classroom floor
and tumbled somewhere far away

(And our teacher taught us a song today...wouldn't you like to hear?)

And I skipped through a day and I skipped through a week
and I hopped through a year, through a year, through a year....

> *"Raspberry, strawberry and apple jam tart...."*

You used to walk home for lunch
consonant sounds growling in your stomach
and your friends scattered with the intersection
the winds sweeping them onto geranium pot porches
and into baked bread flour hands in cookie jar kitchens
your stomach ached with their subtraction

but your street thrust forward, straight on
without a turn, the staff where song notes hung
rounded and red, like little rose blossoms
no shortcuts here, you paused
and watched ants scurry on the concrete, no shortcuts here
you paused, tossed maple seeds and watched them flutter down
no shortcuts here, but shortcuts mark your days now
and your footsteps now, the
cuts,   the c uts,   th e cut s, t   he c ut s...

(And our teacher taught us a song....)

and I skip through a day and I count 1, 2, 3 and
I spell C, A, T and I trace this geography
(right here,   and here,   and here)

    "Raspberry, strawberry, and apple jam tart....."

Because you used to dawdle on your way home for lunch
when autumn rains licked cleanly off
the chalk marks of your childhood games
and your friends would vanish at the intersection
just 1, 2, 3
the ringing of the school bell, clapper
sliding across the smooth skin, cold, metallic, spelling
C, A, T your lessons, the lessons

Because you skipped the morning sidewalk cracks
chanting that nothing would break your mother's back
you asked to be jailed in hopscotch missteps
for just a few minutes more, but the teacher
spilled the pronouns out, and the verbs
pushed you onto the playground and the
asphalt tilted rolling you homeward, with
the autumn wind toying with your coat flaps, its
bone chill touch on your bare legs, and the
tease of the rain, finger-painting leaves
on concrete, tracing crisp shapes, exposing
tendril veins,   the pulsing veins,   the waiting veins

(and our teacher taught us a song, but I forgot the melody, and I can't sing the words)

When your friends were washed away, were the words
you learned to read, were they stubbed out in your brain
were they burned onto the map, did they bloom in red rose
blotches of destination just for today and did you learn
geography in this criss-cross route right
here   and here   and   here   and here

With the ringing of the bell, did you stare past cursive
sentence structured blackboards, did a curtain move aside
did your throat tighten on the words you learned and did you
say just don't be there, just don't be there, just don't…
          sing,   speak,   remember, feel,   and now
if you trace the path down your arm, stub the cigarette out
on that destination, cut out its name, will your friends then
walk you to the door? Come inside? Find tables set, find no
one home, just recite about one dead heart?

>   *"Raspberry, strawberry, apple jam tart*
>   *Find some way past that empty heart*
>   *Raspberry, strawberry, apple jam tart*
>   *tell them the name   tell them the name*

Tell them the name"

V. Lost Coasts & Bare Shelves

Late Autumn in Humboldt

The seasons take their time here
tend to dress casual
slowly remove fog jackets
for an afternoon sun
which reveals that…..sometime
the brown pelicans slipped away south

Contrasts are measured out precisely
the alders that you remember
clinging to green
have let go their foliage into jigsaw shapes
that mat the Mad River's banks
gorging now on the excess
of mountain showers

Breath doesn't venture far
beyond lips, in cold puffs
crisp with early morn that
is beyond examination before
dissipating
at the touch of any sun
poking through

The short range of weather
measures these autumn days
in a moment's blush of ivy
reminisces about the year
through a single lupine
still lingering along the road

Changes come in small doses
you forget when the hydrangea turned brown
you wonder when it was
that you last looked in that direction….

Dusk, Mad River Beach

Sea whips that bring the dunes to heel
with lessons of storms at-hand
and tides to come

Flotsam tales of shores left hanging
at the whim of moments
embellished with seaweed ramblings
soon drowned out by waves' din

Tumble of hills to tidelines
dropping thoughts with tilting of sun
drifting eyeless around a form
that gropes in circles, its feathers torn

Waves frothing at the prospect
of night spilling its ink
with little parchment of beach left
on which to write

A broken wing laden
with the burden of dusk
waiting for stars to skim the sea
promising of skies
still full of flight

Beyond the Fenceline

A calf bucks, wide-eyed
with horizons of cloud bank
and cool, green dozes or nibbles
of the pastured expanses

His nostrils are a bubbling creek
meeting of nose with sweet clover
and banks lavendered with the
soothing smell of lupine

The calf contrasts like a
brown and white throw rug,
a welcome mat for
bounding, sun-warmed afternoons

He raises his heart to the beat
of chases after barn mates
beyond the pulse and safety
shadowed by his mother's bulging flank

The calf's ears scoop air-fulls
of every sound that spring
his hoofs into action
along the puzzlement of fence line

Sounds, of his mother's yank
of grass by the roots
and her steady crunch, and of
the regular "tick," pause, "tick"
static marking tangled, thin wire lines

Beyond which, giving pause

The farmer watches, bemused
but grime-encrusted with the knowledge
of the sanctity of these few moments
and the cruel reality often contained
in all movements forward

Spring, Red Trinities*

a scrum of honeybees
their nest out of bounds
rolls with a punch-drunk
craving for
ultraviolet spread

sun-dressed, manzanita
foams at the mouth
with bloom
a red-veined,
spindly passion for
parched tongue
crisp whispers

spring--a tease
slipping dogwood blooms
up the legs of the
lower slopes

baring peaks
from beneath snow melt
trickling, gurgling under
ribbons of scree
slowly revealed

lizards know this routine
and dart for cover
from the
shooting stars
streaking across
moist, clinging soil

oxidized, in love of
wide valleys
the peaks tumble east, all
red in the face

summer rises there
in steamed haze

Trinity River Daze

Childhood, summer afternoons, when she believed
everything her father told her, like don't swallow
watermelon seeds or one would grow in her stomach,
or that the dark, underwater hole beyond the stream's
marshmallow-shaped boulder, anchoring that particular twist
in the river, that this hole was bottomless

Her father had said this in his serious tone
this being on the Trinity River, where she'd skip stones
across languid summer days and the fish fry would flit
and tickle the gleeful nubs of her toes

She'd drape herself on an inner tube
float as close to that precipice as she dared
wondering what might rise out of the depths
that hoarded all the river's green tint until it was sucked
into a night she imagined twisted, in a passage
that wound through the Earth's bowels
to emerge, as her father had whispered,
somewhere in China, or some other place, far away
somewhere she might venture to some day
to see that water emerge, no longer green
but blue, red or brown or, perhaps, even golden

Then as she paddled to shore, droplets
streaming across her warming skin in the sun
on those afternoons when it blinded, intense and white
from a weighty, blue sky, purged of clouds
she'd see its light fractured into flecks
that glittered in the soft give of the sand

"Fool's gold," her father told her as the lost fortune
stuck to her fingertips and her hopes for riches
tumbled into the river and drifted away
but that night he kissed her forehead
as she still pouted for what was no longer golden

her father whispered about what was most valuable
*"You're worth more than all the gold in the universe.
Never forget that!"*

Staring downstream now, where shallow rapids
pull at her limbs' memory, a dredging machine sucks up the bits
not fooled, pulls up gravel straight from China
chews the Trinity's dazed salmon into ribbons, a shrapnel of
silver and white, hungrily sucks up
those watermelon seeds she spit out over the years,
leaves nothing comforting to be left whispered
in her waterlogged ears

From a lawn chair perch, she dips her toes
into the river, scans a newspaper piece about
someone sickened from the algae bloom
that tints this stream, that green which sucks the last
breath away on this gasping afternoon
she crumples the newspaper piece into her knapsack
it huddles with a sweating block of cheese
some calving Saltines, and a can of cheap beer

Dazed by the light her thoughts fracture, scatter with
the hot breath of the canyon afternoon, they burn and blacken
across the road on the oak-stitched huddling hillsides
where she notes the singed aftermath
of the previous year's wildfires,
hears the flames that hissed and crackled in their furious jumps
at the river, leaving the pines charred and stark

She imagines giant beings and sasquatches, peering across
the jumbled granite outcrops, waiting patiently
for her to close her eyes now so they can slip, unseen
into that bottomless hole that many years ago, she reasoned
had finally had its fill of the spill of gravel, sand
and bite of real fool's gold, once again knowing what her
father had whispered about what to believe
or what not to believe was all just part of the mystery

The Tipping Point
Fields, Oregon, May 2009

"The Earth is unique," sixtyish, shorts and shades man
carefully pumped in with the gas, which he then
topped off with *"Ours is the only planet in the universe
that has any gravity!"*

We'd coasted the tilt of the land from Steens Mountain
to the gates of Fields Station, home of *"world famous"*
hamburgers and retired stockbroker nomads
praising God's tectonic grill
with swipes of dusty film from windshields

This "messenger" seemed determined not to let a grain
escape the forces of salvation, unaware
of our fellow traveler, muttering nearby
"one of those!" with a smirk, a wink, and the fold
of singles into his billfold

Still, I committed to test this man's claim that
the store served the best milkshakes
"…this side of Portland!" even while realizing
so many of the ingredients lay sun-baked
along coils of road, with pancaked rattlers
bisecting the no pass zones for eons and eye blinks

It's no surprise seeing such beliefs
cling to the Earth's rotation in these places
where metal signs oxidize messages
on blistering hot days, their words
shimmering when the shade is rationed
and when the unraveling macadam seems
to radiate all the millions of miles to the sun
in heart palpitations of afternoon

They weigh down all breath, as if
it could sink to the Earth's core, or be funneled

with the landscape into ramshackle focal points
of cracked paint and corrugated tin
then sifted through sagebrush scented gray-green
and late spring grasses that touch lips
with a blinding sheen from the Alvord Desert

They tumble with mid-life crises
through gaps in volcanic tabletops, then rise
over dust-choked valley floors where
giant feet kick at flat tires, dead romances
and missed milk deliveries, gasping at last
before the ancient Gods that rolled nebular cigarettes
across the surrounding plateaus

Later, this man's glimpse of universal secrets
drifted down over our only path, then dissipated
in the rear-view mirror image of Fields Station
a place of pull-tab prophets pumping gas
and bleak store shelves

A place of milkshakes mixed
with ancient tongues, sun-stroke confessions
and a cloying sweetness, poured onto the
blistering blacktop, left behind for the ants to swarm
in a final, blind frenzy

VI. Sun Showers

Singing Lessons

I. Rain Near Uluru*

Swath of cloud floating on the back-breaking load
        of blue depth
a gob of white cream sizzling across the sky skillet

A heat that broils my thoughts into dozing pastels
        one brush stroke painting a dream, sprinkled
        as crystalline pollen of cool, siphoned
        from blinding sun bloom

they're a shoulder tap on the blushing sand
they're a nod to stolid patience, crisp in mulga
        and spinifex
they're a multitude of pores across the ripples of sand
they're a light patter on the straw-shield of my hat
        and a gleam from the Earth's eye

Such moments, the sprinkle of rain
        in a paused desert

II. Performance

The pick-up groans and shakes
        its load of Aboriginal mirth
as the sun bows out gracefully
        in deflating orange
Their laughter teases desert oaks
        into a peripheral motion
        I strain to glimpse

I'm gasping for breath, running
        to better taste the melting landscape
My sweat offered in sacrifice
        and blanketing reason, just a
        mutation writhing
        on the cracked reed of highway
        unable to play a tune

    a ghost drifting
        like a blanched whirlwind
        in the granular sea before Uluru

    a jester seeking
        an appreciative audience
        before dissipating in shadow

III. Katja Juta*-- and Not

wind   moan in crevasse
sandblasted   orange loaf domes   wind
    granite mountain, ten thousand miles away
bird chorus   prickling forest   decades below
    seconds ago   thoughts
single crow in gum tree   sand swirl
    solidified   thoughts   thousands of years gone
tomorrow   stone throw   morning window
    fog creep on hay field   thirty years echoing
calling across   settling as   dew on desert pea
    sky shadow dance   there
here   a moment ago   Katja Juta
    tracing the lines   singing to myself
wind in ears   thoughts scattering   recollected
    under a rustled maple   along a neon street
legible in desert   connecting with the whisper
    of silence

IV. Fall at Tnorala*

Nocturnal shapes evolve
    as clouds coax spurts of lightning
on an elusive horizon, tease
    the slumbering aridity awake

Earthen lips part with anticipation
    of the fine wine squeezed
    from the roiling skies

The wind joins in the game with gusts
        that muffle the ancient cries
as the blanket wrinkles, and is thrown off
        where the star grains are engulfed
        above the yawning theatre of Tnorala

Encouraged by the scene, the thirsting riverbed
        whispers of its snake wriggles
as the gums huddle on the brittle banks
        nodding approval in the long shadows

A cradle tips, and I
        reach across the heavens' expanse
reach for my mother's glittering hands
        and wave to catch my father's searching
        sparkle gaze

Then I'm falling through space
        to the cushion of earth
with a first word forming
        on an awakened tongue

Outside the Boxing Tent
Boulia, Queensland, Australia, April 1992

The outback seeps
        into the sliver of asphalt
Pricking the tire-treaded fingers
        that trace sand grain contours
A futile dust pan
        in this ochre dream immersion

Its shapeless maw
        black and ravenous
Laps at the tidbit
        of a single streetlight, tossed in sacrifice
A humming insect
        of halogen

Across from the wheeze breath
        of a pub, hoarse
        with its pints of dust and drought
Thumps the drumbeat of a town-hopping fair
        pumping its blood
        through the parched tongues of the dry

Straw hats swarm there
        with belt-buckled holds
        on their testosterone spill
As they blow fly swat at
        the nagging thoughts
        swarming around

"Who will take on the 'Brown Bomber?'"
        the pot-bellied mike barks
        at the mating snake wriggles
        of shadow
"Who can go three rounds?"
        and the swarthy dancer near him
        jabs arms that melt this stage
        into his craving for a song line

The "white fellas" swagger
    past the circle of carousel jets
Held in the grounded patterns
    of this moment
And by the pasty and popcorn stand
    that closed curtains hours before
    on the children of daylight

These "ringers" sweat their years
    in a strut to the boxing tent
To be sucked by the challenge
    beneath the canvass flaps
Where blood and alcohol
    and a thousand blows
    will form new words
        on swollen tongues

And beneath where the stars
    that crowd the Southern Cross
Will then emerge renewed
    in this random blotch
        of awareness

Map Folds
Canyon de Chelly, Arizona, April 2006

You hand us a map
        to unfold with early
        morning,
        Somewhere
startling the herd of
        pinon pine
            is the canyon

This trail is marked
        for our convenience
even allowing for
        the drag of our ancestors
        who tear deep grooves
            in the crumble of sand
These bleeding hands of stories
        that nudged forth this landscape

Our ancestors howl
        in our ears,   play loops of
        that song on the car radio
            crackling an insistence
                that it hues this sky

They wreck their four-wheel drives
        on the silence,   insist
            that your licenses be revoked
They import
        boots that tread
        on the hands cupping the landscape
        cracking the finger bones
            in their meditative poses

These boots kick indentations
        in sands that bend the west winds
        into the undulations
            of this awareness of day

We follow arrows,   we
        notice the lone red paintbrush
        burning generations
                across the stolid hint
                        of rock

A dog scampers along the trail
        bored with the routine
                of tourists, but
        wagging its tail
                from a measured distance

We listen for tales from
        the mouth that greets with *"good morning"*
the eyes that fill volumes
        that crack the earth open
        in the voice of canyons
that my ancestors insist
        are wounds
                inoperable

The hands that offer a map
        to fold in back pockets
        of sea crossings, stabbed
        on a compass bearing
the guide that squirms at the edge
        of a precipice, where wings
                flutter on the periphery
                        animate the junipers

You hand us a map
        the folds already coated
                with channels
                        of red dust

Juniper Seeds

A Navajo woman strings juniper seeds
        the discarded sweet of berry
        hardened to a brown slumber
In waiting, they rotate rock spires with sand breath
        puffed into a bowl of sky, they
drop with her needle into the eyebrow raising
        shadow hoard of canyon
        parched with the silent savor of sage
The seeds nestle in swarms of sand
        cracking open welcomes to the sun
content to hold breath
        in pale moonlight

A Navajo woman strings juniper seeds
        lures of berry that alternate
        with the blue beads she condenses from the sky
placing them with sandstone fingers
        and scratching with wind
Her eyes trace across the blanket where she kneels
        poised for a moment on spires
        and the Earth opens, swallowing her gaze
The seeds roll from her fingertips
        into ravines staining days
        with the memory of water
germinating with the unraveling of years
        plying fissures with the touch of her hands

The Navajo woman funnels wind
        to string stars and canyons
        in a silken web poised in the bedrock
and pauses for coyote nose nudging
        brushstrokes of sky
Her eyes affix beyond the curl of her fingers
        a nesting for bluebirds
Her tears glisten, flash flooding the arroyos
        eyes blink with lizard dartings to spaces
        where rock falls need to go

The Navajo woman cuts buttes
        from bands of mesa, spread forth
        in the folds of her blanket
sings of moonrise and solstice points
        to where a juniper may soon grow
        or never grow

The Desecration of Ursa Major*

sleep enthralled, we enter
the soft padding of your realm

there, remembering the
glacial skirting of
trail, eddying along a ridge
then its log-jamming
in a lumbering black
humbled nose dive
into alder thicket

the mystery told in paw prints
asking should you follow, should you go?
where will life burst forth now
beyond the next curve?

what taste will the high bush
blueberries, crowding bedrock,
lure forth?

dream rustler
sniffing the leaves, scattered
before consciousness

oh mother of us all, lost,
lapping the honey of
late summer sky

where is your child, he being
Arcas, now gone four-wheeling
the warm void
eyes turned nova

these turns of road he follows,
noosed in a deliberate line
can only make us cry

dream catcher, releaser of
late day silhouettes,
rubbing eyes of the flash of
alpine meadows we long to roam
crossing our paths
of bear grass flirting
with cumulus dabbed blue, why

full barreled and blind
careening
does your offspring
pursue you into tarred and
feathered
corruptions of sky?

oedipal wreck of
childhood's play, what
gutting of our passage
into glimmerings of night
sucks the dreams out of
these woods, these whispers
of our own eyes watching

oh mother, what is this cold pursuit
and this mutilation*
do they think they can cut out
the very stars
in a purging of sky?
that they will taste of the heavens
in this celestial amputation, the arrogance
seeking to crumple
this arc which carries past
constellations
in a roaming of the heavens?

watch out now, for
we tumble into the void
between one blink of
Ursa Major's eyes
and then we're gone

VII. What to Say

Hold fast to dreams
For when dreams go
Life is a barren field
Frozen with snow.
--- From "Dreams"
by Langston Hughes

Remembering Studs Terkel

The morning oozes
    squeezed, grayish light
    from dirty laundry-heaped
Horizons, my
    head is flat, piss water
    beer and drowned
    then sucked dry
Coffee grounds, somewhere
    I Scrabble spell out
    in my brain
That birds huddle, but will soon sing
    in skeletal branches, their
    wings tightly wrapped
But now I grope
    to shove keys
    in the ignition, and for quarters
In jean pockets, a
    buttonless shirt, balled up
    in the lost and found, seeking
The folding hands of
    some Studs Terkel, or
    his italicized words reminding
That the wrinkles are all
    a part of the wearing

But damn it
    nothing seems to fit at all
    in my dawns anymore

Anagram

when I scramble my letters
I'm an anagram,
then re-assembled
in postage-due moments
and stuck in the midst of a day
I can't recognize
the address, let alone
where to mail
this name

my social security number
got carded for drinking in this life
underage
the pages I ripped
from the library book, long overdue
always left my plot
hanging

reclusive and browned,
I'm pronounced like geraniums
never transplanted
and withering
in the wrung-dry winter light
that settles on dust bunnies
as they reproduce echoes of rooms
in emails to dead friends
wandering whatever
domains
can't ever be found

early one afternoon
around one o'clock or so
my name is rolled with the
bones, skeletal forms
turn up in yellowed pages
telephone calls misdialed
tell me to *"fuck off"*
in accents unfamiliar

to my eardrums
then they hang up

so to escape the w-2's
taxing my patience
and untangle the arms and legs
stuck between bar codes
I hit the road
hoping for answers to click into place
with each number
on the odometer

I downshift Oregon's steep I-5 passes
hoping my silences
will be forgiven, I
give penance at rest stops
fall to my knees
before picnic tables and free
coffee offerings, bitter
with the black taste of
all these cars in idle

I think I hear a word called out
look over my shoulder
the Cascades shrug off letters
in a soup of cumulus language
the summits turn their backs to me
and face the void
speaking in tongues
some unrecognized name
I repeat it in whispers
it tastes of raised dust
burned toast, soured milk
dried blood

I spit it all out
then wait for a sign of
what to say now?
what do I say....

2001: A Kubrick Night at the Accidental Gallery*

Good art isn't any accident, Stanley
    I presume
It sips at a cheap Merlot at one
    in the morning
when the mixed media traipse
    across the room
make advances on the oils
touch privates priced
    with the lack of Discovery

"What do you think you're doing, Dave?"

What's made precise, clean
    pasteurized and mixed with
    Heineken and antidepressants
still leaves felt-penned notes
    saying to use the other door, "Please!"
opens to interpretations
    of car-filled bass and
    wool caps pulled tight
against another night huddled
    in doorways

"Just what do you think you're doing, Dave?"

We should bring in our own
    lawn chairs, we should
pass the brushstrokes hued
    in summer barbecues to cook
    the colors until they crinkle and spit
    protest in their digitized voices
The gallery echoes of the space
    between Friday nights burning pop corn
and Saturday morning, when the smell crescendos
with *"Thus spake Zarathustra"*
    and our artistic sense is reborn

I'm afraid, I'm afraid, Dave...."

The chalice falls to the grime-encrusted
        sidewalk, Stanley
All hands reach out
        to feel the shattered glass
The toasts breed reels of your
        psychedelic edits to wrap 'round
late teenage girls, who circle the building
        polishing rap with their suv's, painting
        angst, that's coughed up
        in cul de sacs, hidden tattoos, and boyfriends
        lost forever inside ill-fitting pants

"I'm afraid, Stanley, my mind is going..."

I cringe as the mc snores, emitting
        pen and inked figures on these
        shadow-gamed walls,
and I still shiver, Stanley,
        as the bone flips upward to the heavens
        four million years pass
but then a cell phone rings out bars
        of beethoven
as your remains sink downward
        from orbit

"My mind is going, there is no question about it...."

This room needs attention, Stanley
Shall we sing it a song?

See there, a lone child sleeps
        on a pallet of bandstand
Maybe he dreams of Strauss waltzes
        dancing across tortured landscapes
Maybe he dreams of a song
        beyond his touch
Maybe that song is   *"Daisy"*

A Free Association in White Without Knowing Spanish

the blank slate, stared at, a moth
flutters across the ceiling, buzz saw noise
cuts through brain's blow-downs, one-by-one
what emerges....blank slate...
"blanco"   the name I offered to my parents
for a samoyed once adopted
from emaciation and abuse

but i don't speak spanish

this holds no significance, the moth
alights in a corner, then melts off a barcelona sun
hung over la rambla,   there, i'm entranced by
a living statue pooling   drop by drop
white on gritty cement

there is no dog in this scene
and i still don't speak spanish

the moth dried in the gritty ceiling cement
a frozen pose, like the snowy egrets, curved into
commas pausing the humboldt bay tides
waiting for me to complete a sentence, a thought
will blanco bound into the muck
chase the birds away?

the blank slate flutters
what's spanish for flight?

carerre, the name for street, not spanish, but catalan
whispered into my ear by a friend
as a taxi sped away with other things
he might have told me, blanco
paused before the living statue, dripping
fish, lures for the egrets, my broom
arm-length toward the victorian ceiling, the moth

not having moved now in days

if i act, with sweeping motions, just a smudge will remind
of its slumber, of the cooking

of shellfish for dinner, several stubborn to open, candle
lit to kill the odor, the moth
awakened and drawn to oratorical
self-destruction   shellfish
a staple in paella,   but i still don't speak spanish
and the smoke curls into a mountainside
forest of spruce
stoked by the dirge march of indian pipe
pale, drooping, monotropa uniflora
that is latin   not spanish
translated in images on the trail, dripping
in the honey late day sunlight, pooling
at the feet of living statues whispering
the name "blanco"

living statues pained with their poses
shifting language, startling

the egret to flight, overhead, scraping clouds of
random thoughts, they rain down on
a gaudi cathedral's unfinished rooms
i'm twisting with a spiral staircase there, rising
above the flame, beyond the broom, yelling the name
"blanco" from a slit of window
where the moth alights

and there is no significance to any of this

i pull on an old shirt, the moth has pockmarked it with holes
my memories slip through each one, freeze
on streets in barcelona, trails in vermont or the cascades
or ambles along a california marsh
everything now renamed, reoccupied by
strange people, speaking in tongues

i don't speak spanish and don't know what....
....had my parents called the dog "blanco,"
just what would have responded
to that name

Burying the Horse

They say that this spot
      in the field
         will eventually be
            depressed

But now
      it's just a chaotic
      upturning of earth
      amidst tangles
         of blue vetch and clover

From here you can see
      the barn   gaping
         its doors wide open

The barn, with its plains
      of grime-packed floorboard
      and darkness glued
         to sweet spears of hay

The barn, where
      the only sounds now
      are of flies buzzing
         over dried, streaks of fluids

      And the hint of groans, monotone
      and thick with
         humid, July afternoons

The Granite Coffee House
Woody Point, Newfoundland, August 2018

I'm guessing that the granite
in the café's name is
related to Newfie pride
Or a nod to the Long Range
Mountains, rising from the wind-whipped
bay beyond, such
Clichés and the obvious
going down easy with the
unexpected foam patterns
of my latte

After all, this is a place where
winter drums its Arctic-tuned fingers
in the rhythm of the stunted black spruce
And mats of tuckamore, reminding
all growth to know its place
A bitter season that scrapes
at the barren plateaus
well into May most years, whispering
"I'll soon be back"

I'm thinking that the name's a nod to
great uncles and grandfathers never known
giving advice from the bottom of
The inlets where
gale-whipped snow
hid the thin ice and to
Women pleading in
pitch black and near headlands
their fading cries
swallowed into the wind
and crashing waves, it's

Unplanned knocks on doors
weighted with the heavy stones
of harsh news,
confusing the odd hours, and it's

The cheerful, colored
façade of chained-to-bedrock
homes, beckoning to
heaving fishing boats
too often just
out of reach

When I inquire about the café's name
I learn though, that granite is
not the prevalent rock here
at all, the landscape instead
A hodge-podge, a puzzle
of interlocking, breaking, transforming, accumulating
years and ages, the rocks a mix of
Sedimentary, igneous
and metamorphic

It seems that the Basques, the
French, all Europeans who fished these
waters over many centuries would
Lug granite stones from overseas
to use as ballast, thus
dropping them overboard as
The fish were hauled in
so as to keep things in balance
to keep all from
possibly sinking

I look out onto Bonne Bay, thirty-five years
since my last trek to this village
on "The Rock," when
I knew nothing of lattes, the internet or
What lay at the bottom
of the waters beyond,
helping to partially frame Gros Morne and the Tablelands
Not knowing then of this
resting place for
so much extra weight
that needed to be
left behind

Porch Gathering

There is the feel and smell
of humidity, the August air
pressing down on the porch roof
and our shoulders, both sagging under
summer surfeit and passing years
notched, ringed and crevassed

A smell and sounds bursting
with the last, lush green, hormone memory
of songbird territorial high notes and
children pitching screams as
they race across
distant fields, into the shadowed mysteries
of white pine groves, there is

This smell, a distinct weight of
acres of kernels, stalks, tassels
sweet with the season, perhaps
too sickeningly so, maybe overloading
taste buds with something that settles
out of sight, hinting at bitter, even of things
rank growing, or buried, beyond the wraparound
porch, within or beyond
the property lines, there is

The view
of a drooped, electrical line, tying
house to road, there is
the flicking, bobbing tail of
a flycatcher that landed there, something drawing
the eyes, a distraction, a
conversation piece
for a single moment, there is

The tone of small talk, overburdened like
whole notes falling into
the lawn grass below, fighting

dissonance, breaking into desperate
halves, quarters, eighths, there is
the hum and whir
of movements both familiar
and threatening, what is it
that goes up and down, back
and forth, ticks by, arcs, then catches
each eye? There is

A sound
the chirruping of crickets
herding the undergrowth
towards brown and autumn
the vacuum suck towards horizons, lights
paling, dreams deflating
the places that were once reflected
and framed and told in
folding chair conversations, a sound
tickling under the skin, wearing out its
elasticity, stretching, pulling
all ears to that point
between the rubbing of cricket
legs, dry, cracked, at a loss
for anything else to say, there is

The distance between where we sit
measuring, counting, glancing
down the parched, dirt road, wishing
for the raising of dust, any distraction
from what is coming, what has been
what might have been
what is left to say, or never
to be said

Deja View
In the Trinity Alps, California, August 2009

I.
bow of moon
curving into dusk
  caught in a lure of douglas fir
  spinning its tales of canyon days
with a turn of my head
its story concludes, the sliver of moon
  slips into space, pricks the skin of sky
  bends into the night
it shoots the evening star forth
to speed its words
  past the slumping granite peaks
the notes sail through dreams
  of the light years
in the morning their melody
  awakens me
  in dew drops of dawn

II.
i once read that over a lifetime
you're likely to breath in the same molecules
  atoms, sub-atomic particles
and tidbits of sunset, the same ingredients
that were inhaled by the millions, the
  billions before you
you're likely to breath in something
  that passed by the nostril hairs of an aristotle
galileo or helen keller, that was perfumed
  with the sweet of a goblet of wine at lips
  acrid with the hint of gunpowder on cratered pastures
that pinched venus and moon cycles
  between fingers, placed rings
around saturn, over a lifetime
you may cough up bits, gagging and nauseous with
  the rantings of a hitler, sneeze with satisfaction
a bar of mozart or a langston hughes line
while gazing at a frozen field,

taste the wild strawberries
  that tanged the tongue of emily dickenson
the slice of moon
  garnishing her plate of heavens
over a lifetime you're likely to
  touch the moment
when this very universe was set loose
feel the sprinkling of the stars
  into murmur and chime and song
of stream, seeking distant sands
  on familiar shores

III.
i perspire into
the drift of fog
remembering balsam needles
and haircap moss sips
of my long effort, i
trickle down granite slabs
inviting the grains from each journey
to join with me, steep
with the tannic brown
of spruce root in ponds, gather
tales of trees, from wind-dropped
seed to towering redwood
and the boulders
yet to tumble
into the curve of glacial notch
braid them into landscapes
where my footsteps will fall
some day

now to drink
of these distant spaces
now to ponder
of where i once left such thoughts
hanging on a crescent moon, perched
on another sky

Early April

Tufted titmouse
greets crest of
orange sunlight
peeking over Mt. Moosilauke

His rapid exclamation
in threes, a frenzied
waltz, calving clock
or avian version
of some holy trilogy

If this single note
bug-fed
with nested
first lessons

Were it a word
thrice repeated
what would it be?

My day's initial question lingers
on this chill morning when
winter won't budge
for April fools

It mutters in white flecks
dusting restless browns of
the matted grass, hollowed
milkweed stalk and
stubble of cornfield
wanting to be scratched, spread
beyond this picture window

Spring seems lost to me
but songbirds know the score
and tufted titmouse
has spoken

I wonder, is the word, repeated
"wake, wake, wake"
or *"here, here, here"*
or *"time, time, time….."*

Who decides?
Now….

Notes

Hand-written quote by the buyer of a book by Franz Wright. The buyer gave it as a gift. The book was found in a used bookstore in Arcata, California.

The Trinities are a range of mountains in Trinity County, California and are commonly divided into the Green, White & Red Trinities.

Uluru is the Aboriginal name for what is said to be the largest piece of exposed rock in the world, located in the Northern Territory of Australia. Europeans named it "Ayer's Rock."

Katja Juta is the Aboriginal name for a formation of sandstone domes about 20 miles west of Uluru. Europeans named them the "Olgas."

Tnorala is the Aboriginal name for a formation in Australia's Northern Territory named "Gosse Bluff" by Europeans. It is a crater that is said to have been created by a comet hitting the Earth 142 million years ago. According to the Aboriginal people, it was formed in the creation time when a group of women danced across the Milky Way. One mother's baby rested in a wooden carrier which tipped, causing the baby to drop to the Earth.

A Roman myth involves both bears, Ursa Major and Ursa Minor. The god Jupiter was smitten by the maiden, Callisto. This made Jupiter's wife, Juno, jealous and when Callisto gave birth to a son Juno guessed that the father was Jupiter. She decided to turn Callisto into a bear so she would no longer be attractive. The son, named Arcas, grew up to be a hunter. One day he was hunting in the forest and Callisto was so excited to see him that she ran up to him, forgetting she was a bear. Arcas shot an arrow at his mother, but Jupiter stopped it from hitting Callisto.

Bears are regularly poached and mutilated for the illegal trade in their body parts, which are "prized" in various countries in Asia.

The Accidental Gallery used to be an art gallery in Eureka, CA.

www.ingramcontent.com/pod-product-compliance
Lightning Source LLC
Chambersburg PA
CBHW020144130526
44591CB00030B/208